Bible
Promises
made easy

Mark Water

Bible Promises Made Easy
Hendrickson Publishers, Inc.
P.O. Box 3473
Peabody, Massachusetts 01961-3473

Copyright © 2001
John Hunt Publishing
Text copyright © 2001 Mark Water

ISBN 1-56563-623-6

Designed and produced
by Tony Cantale Graphics

First printing — October 2001

Manufactured in Hong Kong/China

Photography supplied by
Artville, Digital Stock, Digital
Vision, Goodshoot, Photo Alto,
Photodisc and Tony Cantale

Illustrations by
Tony Cantale Graphics

Contents

Special pull-out chart
Over 200 Bible promises to meditate on

When I need God's blessing

Bible Promise No. 1
"The generation of the upright will be blessed."
Psalm 112:2

Looking at the context
One way to appreciate God's promises is to search them out in the Bible and note their surrounding verses. Often the verses close to a verse containing a promise from God will shed light on its meaning. There is danger in isolating any Bible verse from its context. A text out of context can easily become a pretext for saying something other than what the verse means.

The context of Psalm 112:2
"Praise the Lord.
Blessed is the man who fears the Lord,
* who finds great delight in his*
*   commands.*
His children will be mighty in the land;
* the generation of the upright will be*
*   blessed.*
Wealth and riches are in his house,
* and his righteousness endures forever.*
Even in darkness light dawns for the
*   upright,*
* for the gracious and compassionate*
*   and righteous man."*
Psalm 112:1-4

Blessings from above
We all would like to receive blessing after blessing from God. These verses give one of the ways that the Bible states this is possible. We are to "fear the Lord."

Verse 1 shows the meaning of "fear of the Lord" – people who "fear" God find "great delight in his commands." This fear does not mean to cower from God, rather, it means to reverence him; to treat him with respect and awe, and desire to please him.

People who "fear" God in this way are "upright," because they keep his laws.

When I face adversity

Finding God in adversity

"In all trouble you should seek God. You should not set him over against your troubles, but within them. God can only relieve your troubles if you in your anxiety cling to him. Trouble should not really be thought of as this thing or that in particular, for our whole life on earth involves trouble; and through the troubles of our earthly pilgrimage we find God."

Augustine of Hippo

Three things to remember

• You are created
In times of trouble, says Isaiah, remember who created you.
"But now, this is what the Lord says – he who created you."
Isaiah 43:1

• You are redeemed
In times of trouble, the Lord says,
"Fear not, for I have redeemed you."
Isaiah 43:1

• You are summoned, that is called by name
In times of trouble, the Lord says,
"Fear not ... I have summoned you by name; you are mine."
Isaiah 43:1

Bible Promise No. 2

"When you pass through the waters, I will be with you; and when you pass through the rivers, they will not sweep over you. When you walk through the fire, you will not be burned; the flames will not set you ablaze."
Isaiah 43:2

5

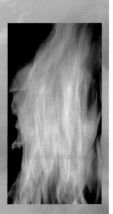

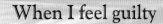

When I feel guilty

Bible Promise No. 3

"Come now, let us reason together," says the Lord. "Though your sins are like scarlet, they shall be as white as snow; though they are red as crimson, they shall be like wool."
Isaiah 1:18

1. Sins like scarlet

Isaiah had in mind the deep scarlet and purple dye which the Phoenicians made from the juice of the murex shellfish off the coast of Palestine. The shells were crushed, cooked in salt, and left in the sun where their secretions turned purple.

This dye was so effective that once the tissues of any garment were impregnated with murex juice, the color could never be washed out.

2. The deduction

If we sincerely seek God's forgiveness no sin is too big to be forgiven.

3. "The treasures of the snow"

"Once God preached to me by a similitude in the depth of winter. There earth had been black, and there was scarcely a green thing or a flower to be seen.

As I looked across the fields, there was nothing but barrenness – bare hedges and leafless trees, and black earth, wherever I gazed. On a sudden God spake, and unlocked the treasures of the snow, and white flakes descended until there was no blackness to be seen, and all was one sheet of dazzling whiteness.

It was at that time that I was seeking the Savior, and not long before I found Him, and I remember well that sermon which I saw before me in the snow: 'Come now, and let us reason together, saith the Lord: though your sins be as scarlet, they shall be white as snow; though they be red like crimson, they shall be as wool.'"
C.H. Spurgeon

When things go wrong

Looking for the promise
In the Bible, promises from God are linked to, and rest on, statements about God. We trust the promises because of who God is.

The great statement about God in this verse is that God is sovereign. "The Sovereign Lord ... ." It is essential to remember this whenever disaster strikes or a crisis looms.

7

Bible Promise No. 4

*"The Sovereign Lord is my strength;
he makes my feet like the feet of a deer,
he enables me to go on the heights."*
Habakkuk 3:19

Looking at the problem
The Bible always encourages us to face reality and not hide from problems. Habakkuk had to face the prospect of famine.

**"Though the fig tree does not bud
   and there are no grapes on the vines.
though the olive crop fails
   and the fields produce no food,
though there are no sheep in the pen
   and no cattle in the stalls,
yet I will rejoice in the Lord,
   I will be joyful in God my Savior."**
   Habakkuk 2:17-18

Looking to the Lord
Habakkuk is saying that God enables him to surmount every difficulty. This is because his happiness is not dependent on the circumstances but on God, who is his Savior.

The frost of adversity
"Christian, remember the goodness of God in the frost of adversity."
   C.H. Spurgeon

When I'm in trouble

Bible Promise No. 5

"Then they cried out to the Lord in their trouble, and he brought them out of their distress.
He stilled the storm to a whisper; the waves of the sea were hushed."
Psalm 107:28-29

What should we do when we're in trouble?

• Pray

When in trouble one's reaction may be to fret and worry, but a Christian's instinctive reaction should be to pray. As the psalmist states: "they cried out to the Lord in their trouble." What we do in a crisis uncovers our spiritual state.

• Express our trust

We show our trust in God by praying to him. Even when we are at our wits end, the psalmist encourages us to cry out to God. If we are feeling desperate, we should tell God that this is how we feel as we "cry out" to him.

• Remember God's power

When in trouble, remember Psalm 107:28-29 – these verses reveal God's power. Commentating on this passage, Leslie C. Allen has written, "God's power is a match for any crisis."

Trust

Trust in yourself and you are doomed to disappointment.
Trust in your friends and they will die and leave you.
Trust in money and you may have it taken away from you.
Trust in reputation and some slanderous tongues will blast it.
But trust in God and you are never to be confounded in time or in eternity.
  Dwight L. Moody

When I want to praise God

Note what's on the psalmist's list

God is:
- My Rock
- My loving God
- My fortress
- My stronghold
- My deliverer
- My shield
- My refuge

Israel was a war-torn land, frequently attacked by vicious and violent aggressors. The psalmist drew his images of God from his own experiences. God provided the psalmist a place of complete safety and security.

How to write your own psalm

Make a shortlist about God – what does he mean to you?

Having read your own list about God, and having read the Psalmist's list, you can then do what the psalmist did – praise God.

Go through some of God's characteristics on your list and give thanks to God. The psalmist would have prayed from his list, "Thank you God that you are my shield."

In this way you will be writing your own psalm of praise.

Models for praise

"The best models for our praise are found in the psalms."
Lawrence O. Richards

Bible Promise No. 6

"Praise be to the Lord my Rock, ... He is my loving God and my fortress, my stronghold and my deliverer, my shield in whom I take refuge ..."
Psalm 144:1-2

9

When I need comfort

Bible Promise No. 7
"I, even I, am he who comforts you."
Isaiah 51:12

Promises in the Hebrew of the Old Testament

Often, in the Old Testament, the English translation of the Hebrew words says that somebody promised something. But in the Hebrew it simply says that someone said or spoke something.

Throughout the Old Testament we are taught that when God speaks the action is as good as done.

So when God declares in Isaiah, "I am he who comforts you," this is God's promise that he does and will comfort.

Like a caring shepherd
*"He tends his flock like a shepherd:
He gathers the lambs in his arms
and carries them close to his heart;
he gently leads those that have young."*
Isaiah 40:11

Comfort and joy
*"I will turn their mourning into
gladness;
I will give them comfort and joy instead
of sorrow."*
Jeremiah 31:13

Sources of comfort
*"I beseech you do not treat God's
promises as if they were curiosities for a
museum; but use them as everyday
sources of comfort."*
C.H. Spurgeon

When I need comfort

How does God comfort us?

• With himself
Through the Bible we get to know God. God himself is the primary source of all comfort. He is the "God of all comfort."

• Through physical things
After his confrontation with the prophets of Baal on Mount Hermon and his great victory, Elijah fled in fear of his life. As depression sank in, he fled into the desert where he prayed for death. Exhausted he fell asleep. An angel woke Elijah and provided him with hot bread, baking over a fire, and fresh water. See 1 Kings 19:5-7

"Strengthened by that food, he traveled for forty days and nights until he reached Horeb, the mountain of God." 1 Kings 19:8

• Through people
God continually comforted Paul with human friendship. We rightly think of Paul as being a super-spiritual giant, but God used a relatively inexperienced Christian to convey God's comfort to this pioneer missionary.

"But God, who comforts the downcast, comforted us by the coming of Titus ..." 2 Corinthians 7:6

Passing on God's comfort
When God comforts us, we can share that experience. Paul wrote that he had been comforted ...

"... so that we can comfort those in any trouble with the comfort we ourselves have received from God." 2 Corinthians 1:4

Bible Promise No. 8

"Praise be to the God and Father of our Lord Jesus Christ, the Father of compassion and the God of all comfort, who comforts us in all our troubles ..."
2 Corinthians 1:3-4

11

When I'm at a low ebb

Bible Promise No. 9

"... the Lord gives sight to the blind, the Lord lifts up those who are bowed down, the Lord loves the righteous. The Lord watches over the alien and sustains the fatherless and the widow ..."
Psalm 146:8-9

What does God promise and to whom?

God promises specific help for definite problems.

Our problems	God's provision
1. Inability to see (This may be physical or spiritual)	Sight – "The Lord gives sight ..."
2. A feeling of being oppressed or weighed down	The burden is taken away or we are given strength to look up and carry it.
3. Alienation, loneliness	God's presence – God smiles at us, even when others turn their backs on us. "The Lord watches over ..."
4. Poverty or fear of poverty	Provision for physical and material needs – "The Lord sustains ..."

Weakness

Don't be upset about being weak. The English missionary, Gladys Aylward, traveled to China on her own without the backing of any missionary society. Near the end of her life she wrote:

"I have two planks for a bed, two stools, two cups and a basin. On my broken wall is a small card which says, 'God hath chosen the weak things – I can do all things through Christ who strengthens me.' It is true I have passed through fire."

When I need God's strength

Martin Luther

In the middle of the turbulent days of the Reformation, Martin Luther was fighting to re-establish biblical truth. Often in danger of imprisonment and death, he composed a hymn based on the opening verses of Psalm 46.

A safe stronghold

A safe stronghold our God is still,
* A trusty shield and weapon;*
He'll help us clear from all the ill
* That hath now o'ertaken. ...*
And though they take our life,
* Goods, honor, children, wife,*
* Yet is their profit small;*
* These things shall vanish all:*
The City of God remaineth!
    Martin Luther, translated by Thomas Carlyle

"Let us sing the 46th Psalm"

Luther published his hymn in 1529. The words and music soon spread over Germany. These words strengthened Luther during some of the darkest hours of his life. Luther would often say to his friend Melanchthon, "Come, Philip, let us sing the 46th Psalm."

When Melanchthon and his two friends were banished from Wittenberg in 1547, they were greatly comforted when they heard a little girl singing this hymn in the street. "Sing on, dear daughter," Melanchton said, "thou knowest not what great people thou art now comforting."

Bible Promise No. 10

"God is our refuge and strength, an ever-present help in trouble. Therefore we will not fear, though the earth give way and the mountains fall into the heart of the sea."
Psalm 46:1-2

When I'm being persecuted

Bible Promise No. 11

"And the God of all grace, who called you to his eternal glory in Christ, after you have suffered a little while, will himself restore you and make you strong, firm and steadfast."
1 Peter 5:10

Note what God does NOT promise

Peter wrote his first letter to encourage Christians who were being persecuted. Peter does not say that they will never have to suffer persecution.

Note what God DOES promise

• **The duration of suffering**
This will not be unending. It is only for "a little while."
It contrasted with their "glory in Christ" which is "eternal."

• **Restoration will come**
"God ... himself will restore you."
The word Peter uses here for "restore" is the word used for setting a broken bone, and for equipping and arranging a fleet of ships ready for battle.
So there is a double meaning here:

1. God will provide for everything that is necessary to see you through any persecution.
2. God will repair anything that is damaged.

God's promise of bliss

In his commentary on this verse, G.J. Polkinghorne has written: "The surest source of strength is found in the personal interest of God and his promise of eternal bliss."

Peace in suffering

"Either God will shield you from suffering or he will give you unfailing strength to bear it. Be at peace, then, and put aside all anxious thoughts and imaginings."
Francis de Sales

When I'm in danger

The Treasury of David

The great English Baptist preacher, C.H. Spurgeon, spent 21 years reading, researching, and writing his commentary on the Psalms which he called *The Treasury of David*. Commenting on Psalm 121:3 he wrote:

The paths of life
"Though the paths of life are dangerous and difficult, yet we shall stand fast, for Jehovah will not permit our feet to slide; and if he will not suffer it we shall not suffer it."

Feet, head, and heart
"If our feet will be thus kept we may be sure that our head and heart will be preserved also."

Promised preservation
In the original Hebrew the words express a wish or prayer – "May he not suffer your foot to be moved." Our preservation should be the subject of perpetual prayer.

"He ... will not slumber"

By day and by night
"We should not stand a moment if our keeper were to sleep; we need him by day and by night; not a single step can be taken except under his guardian eye."
  C.H. Spurgeon

Divine bodyguard
"God is the bodyguard of his saints. No fatigue or exhaustion can cast our God into sleep; his watchful eyes are never closed." C.H. Spurgeon

Bible Promise No. 12
"He will not let your foot slip— he who watches over you will not slumber."
Psalm 121:3

When I despair

The book of Lamentations

Few individual Christians or groups of Christians are called to experience the events described in the book of Lamentations.

In 587 BC God's people faced a bottomless pit of despair when Nebuchadnezzar's army besieged, starved, and destroyed Jerusalem. As they were led off to Babylon, they felt that they had lost everything – including God. They had lost:

• their holy city
• their place of worship – the temple
• their homes
• their livelihood
• their freedom
• their sense of God's protecting love

A sandwich of despair

Lamentations 3:22-23 is deliberately placed in the middle of a sandwich of despair. Before these verses and then following, the horrors endured by the devastated people of Jerusalem are graphically described. This was a device often used in Hebrew poetry. In order to emphasize that this terrible time was also a time of hope, Jeremiah deliberately places these verses of hope in the middle of his bitter laments over fallen Jerusalem.

Hope

"To live without hope is to cease to live."
Fyodor Dostoevsky

"It is impossible for that man to despair who remembers that his helper is omnipotent."
Jeremy Taylor

When I stumble

The two ways
Psalm 37 contrasts the way of the wicked and the way of the righteous. The psalmist shows us how to live a life which pleases God – a life in the Spirit.

A promise for the few
Verses 23-24 are only for those in whom the Lord delights. They are those who:
• trust in God *v.3*
• do good *vs.3,27*
• delight in God *v.4*
• refrain from anger *vs.8,37*
• live by God's word *v.31*
• do not take things into their own hands *vs.7,34*

"If the Lord delights in a man's way, he makes his steps firm; though he stumble, he will not fall, for the Lord upholds him with his hand."
Psalm 37:23-24

Steps
"God does not always show his servants his way for a distance, but leads them step by step, as children are led."
Matthew Henry

When a Christian loved one dies

Bible Promise No. 15

"He will wipe every tear from their eyes. There will be no more death or mourning or crying or pain, for the old order of things has passed away."
Revelation 21:4

It's natural to experience sadness

When a Christian friend or relative dies it is natural to feel keenly the loss of their love and friendship. Christians should be the first to "mourn with those who mourn," as Paul states in Romans 12:15.

Life beyond this life

However, Christians believe that there is more to life than this earthly world. The great sadness for non-Christians is that, for them, there is nothing beyond this world. Paul pointed out that if Christians limit their Christian faith to this life they are sad people indeed.

"If only for this life we have hope in Christ, we are to be pitied more than all men." Romans 15:19

A picture of heaven

When a Christian loved one dies we should attempt to focus on their joy in heaven rather than on our feelings of loss.

In heaven God "will wipe every tear from their eyes" because the causes for crying are removed.

In heaven there is:
- no more death
- [no more] mourning
- [no more] crying
- [no more] pain

"for the old order of things has passed away."

Believing God's promises

"What greater rebellion, impiety, or insult to God can there be, than not to believe his promises?" Martin Luther

When I need God's presence

Enfolded by love

When a baby is upset he may contort his face, clench his fists, and scream. Then the mother picks up her child, enfolding her baby with her love, and quietly sings until he is soothed.

That's how God wishes to be with us.

Praying for God's presence

Columba, the sixth century Irish missionary to Scotland, wrote this prayer asking for God's presence to be with him.

"Be thou a bright flame before me,
Be thou a guiding star above me,
Be thou a smooth path below me,
Be thou a kindly shepherd behind me,
Today – tonight – and forever."
Columba of Iona

Bible Promise No. 16

"The Lord your God is with you, he is mighty to save.
He will take great delight in you, he will quiet you with his love, he will rejoice over you with singing."
Zephaniah 3:17

Bible Promise No. 17

"He [the living God] rescues and he saves; he performs signs and wonders in the heavens and on the earth."
Daniel 6:27

What a tragedy!
In the days of Jeremiah, God's people had been overwhelmed by disaster after disaster. They had turned their backs on God. As a result a godless nation had invaded and defeated them, and then carried them off as prisoners.

They left behind the holy city of Jerusalem and were cut off from the temple. It seemed as if they been deserted by God.

Daniel was among those deported to Babylon but did not waver in his faith nor in his love for God.

Isaiah prophesied that God would comfort his people in this tragedy.

"Comforted over Jerusalem"

*"For this is what the Lord says: ... you will ... be carried on her arm and dandled on her knees.
As a mother comforts her child, so will I comfort you; and you will be comforted over Jerusalem."*
Isaiah 66:12-13

Personal tragedy

"May I accept God's will not with dumb resignation, but with holy joy; not only with the absence of murmur, but with a song of praise." George Matheson, who became blind and was disappointed in love

When tragedy hits

Personal tragedy
"My little daughter Elizabeth is dead. She has left me wonderfully sick at heart and almost womanish, I am so moved by pity for her. I could never have believed a father's heart could be so tender for his child. Pray to God for me." Martin Luther

Trust and tragedy
Personal tragedies strike Christians just as much as everyone else. What should differentiate Christians from everyone else is our reaction to tragedies.

While it may be a "normal" reaction to blame other people or to blame God for a tragedy, Christians are taught to take another approach. We are to trust God despite tragedy and even during tragedy.

The trust that we may hold
In God alone there is faithfulness and faith in the trust that we may hold to him, to his promise and to his guidance. To hold to God is to rely on the fact that God is there for me, and to live in this certainty." Karl Barth

"And we know that in all things God works for the good of those who love him, who have been called according to his purpose."
Romans 8:28

When I need God's peace

Bible Promise No. 19

[Jesus said] "I have told you these things, so that in me you may have peace. In this world you will have trouble. But take heart! I have overcome the world."
    John 16:33

Some secrets of true peace

1. Peace comes from trusting in Jesus' death
"God presented him [Jesus] as a sacrifice of atonement, through faith in his blood. ... Therefore, since we have been justified through faith, we have peace with God through our Lord Jesus Christ."
    Romans 3:25; 5:1

2. Peace comes from following God's will
"I desire to do your will, O my God; your law is within my heart."
    Psalm 40:8

3. Peace comes from the God of peace
"For God is not a God of disorder but of peace." *1 Corinthians 14:33*

Peace in the writing of Isaiah

1. Peace comes from trusting God
*"You will keep in perfect peace
    him whose mind is steadfast,
    because he trusts in you."*
    Isaiah 26:3

2. Peace is a gift from God
*"Lord, you establish peace for us;
    all that we have accomplished you have
        done for us."*
    Isaiah 26:12

3. "Peace" is one of Jesus' names
*"And he will be called Wonderful
        Counselor, Mighty God,
Everlasting Father, Prince of Peace."*
    Isaiah 9:6

4. God's peace is to flood our hearts
"I will extend peace to her like a river."
    Isaiah 66:12

When I need God's forgiveness

Martin Luther's dream

Martin Luther once recounted a dream he had. In the dream there was a book where all Luther's sins were written. The devil spoke to Luther, "Martin, here is one of your sins, here is another," pointing to the writing in the book. Then Luther said to the devil, "Take a pen and write, 'The blood of Jesus Christ, God's Son, cleanses us from all sin.'" *See 1 John 1:7.*

Bible Promise No. 20
"If we confess our sins, he is faithful and just and will forgive us our sins and purify us from all unrighteousness."
1 John 1:9

Going astray

"How ready we are to go astray! How easily we are drawn aside into innumerable snares, while in the meantime we are bold and confident, and doubt not but we are right and safe! How much do we stand in need of the wisdom, the power, the condescension, patience, forgiveness, and gentleness of our good Shepherd!"
Jonathan Edwards

Forgiveness

"1 TREE + 3 NAILS = 4 GIVEN"
Author unknown

"When Christ's hands were nailed to the cross, he also nailed your sins to the cross."
Bernard of Clairvaux

When I need renewal

Bible Promise No. 21

*"Praise the Lord,
O my soul,
and forget not all
his benefits—
who forgives all
your sins
and heals all your
diseases,
who redeems your
life from the pit
and crowns you
with love and
compassion,
who satisfies your
desires with
good things
so that your youth
is renewed like
the eagle's."*
Psalm 103:2-5

The eagle

The psalmist tells us that when we are ill
– physically, emotionally or spiritually –
God heals and renews us. Like the
psalmist, the prophet Isaiah draws on the
image of the powerful eagle. Everyone
grows tired and weak, even healthy young
men, but there is a way of recovering
inner vitality.

*"Even youths grow tired and weary,
    and young men stumble and fall;
but those who hope in the Lord
    will renew their strength.
They will soar on wings like eagles;
    they will run and not grow weary,
    they will walk and not be faint."*
    Isaiah 40:30

When I'm full of God's love

The chapter of love

1 Corinthians chapter 13 has been called the "greatest love poem" in the world.
In verses 4-7, seven things that love does are listed, and seven things that love does not do are also listed.

Love is	Love does not, is not
1. Love is patient *v.4*	Love does not envy *v.4*
2. Love is kind *v.4*	Love does not boast *v.4*
3. Love rejoices in the truth *v.6*	Love is not proud *v.4*
4. Love always protects *v.7*	Love is not rude *v.5*
5. Love always trusts *v.7*	Love is not self-seeking *v.5*
6. Love always hopes *v.7*	Love is not easily angered *v.5*
7. Love always perseveres *v.7*	Love does not delight in evil *v.6*

Eight promises in three verses

In response to our love for God, God gives eight promises in three verses.

"'Because he loves me,'" says the Lord,
1. *'I will rescue him;*
2. *I will protect him, for he acknowledges my name.*
3. *He will call upon me, and I will answer him;*
4. *I will be with him in trouble,*
5. *I will deliver him*
6. *and honor him;*
7. *With long life will I satisfy him*
8. *and show him my salvation.'"*
   Psalm 91:14-16

Bible Promise No. 22

"'Though the mountains be shaken and the hills be removed, yet my unfailing love for you will not be shaken nor my covenant of peace removed,' says the Lord, who has compassion on you."
Isaiah 54:10

25

When I'm being tempted

Bible Promise No. 23

"No temptation has seized you except what is common to man. And God is faithful; he will not let you be tempted beyond what you can bear. But when you are tempted, he will also provide a way out so that you can stand up under it."

1 Corinthians 10:13

The pattern of temptation

Knowing the tactics of our enemy helps us to defeat him.

Pattern	Eve: *Genesis 3:6*	Jesus: *Matthew 4:1-11*
1. The look	Eve saw the fruit	Jesus was asked to look at all the kingdoms
2. The desire	Eve desired to eat the fruit	Jesus had the desire to eat, as he was so hungry
3. The taking	Eve took the fruit	Jesus was tempted to take his life in his own hands and throw himself from the top of the temple

Temptations and trials

"In all temptations and trials we have God's promises to rest our souls upon."
Matthew Henry

Remember that Jesus could come at any time

"For the grace of God ... teaches us to say no to ungodliness and worldly passions, and to live self-controlled, upright and godly lives ... while we wait ... for the glorious appearing of our great God and Savior."
Titus 2:11-13

"I do not think that in the last forty years I have lived one conscious hour that was not influenced by the thought of our Lord's return."
Lord Shaftesbury

When I'm being tempted

Being tempted is not the same as committing sin

We know this is true because Jesus was sinless, yet he was tempted.

"... we have one who has been tempted in every way, just as we are–yet was without sin." Hebrews 4:15

Avoiding temptation

"He that will play with Satan's bait, will quickly be taken with Satan's hook."
  Thomas Brooks

"Temptation usually comes in through a door that has deliberately been left open." Author unknown

"The best way to overcome temptation is to avoid the tempting situation."
  Author unknown

Knowing what tempts you

"Be thoroughly acquainted with your temptations and the things that may corrupt you – and watch against them all day long. You should watch especially the most dangerous of the things that corrupt, and those temptations that either your company or business will unavoidably lay before you."
  Richard Baxter

Temptations and trials

*The devil tempts that he may ruin;
God tests that he may crown.*
  Ambrose

Bible Promise No. 24

"Because he [Jesus] himself suffered when he was tempted, he is able to help those who are being tempted."
  Hebrews 2:18

Victory with Jesus

He said not:

*"Thou shalt not be tempted:
Thou shalt not be travailed:
Thou shalt not be afflicted."*

But he said:

"Thou shalt not be overcome."
  Julian of Norwich

When I want to prosper

In the eyes of the world
In the eyes of the world prosperity means success and wealth. How one achieves that "success" is not usually questioned.

In the eyes of God
In the eyes of God prosperity means to live in love and peace, and with God and one's neighbor. It comes about as a result of:

1. Obedience to God
"We are God's glory, when we follow his ways."
    Florence Nightingale

2. Being faithful to God
In the parable of the talents Jesus used exactly the same words to commend that servant who had used wisely the five talents as he did when he commended the servant who had used wisely only two talents.
"Well done, good and faithful servant! You have been faithful with a few things; I will put you in charge of many things. Come and share your master's happiness."
    Matthew 25:21, and 23

Likeness to Jesus
Jesus is the fulfilment of God's law.
"It is not great talents God blesses so much as great likeness to Jesus. A holy minister is an awful weapon in the hand of God."
    Robert Murray M'Cheyne

When I want to defeat the devil

1. Vigilant

"The tendency of all that Scripture teaches concerning the devil is to put us on our guard against his wiles and machinations, that we may provide ourselves with weapons strong enough to drive away the most formidable of foes. For when Satan is called the god and ruler of this world, the strong man armed, the prince of the power of the air, the roaring lion, the object of all these descriptions is to make us more cautious and vigilant, and more prepared for the contest."

John Calvin

2. Take the initiative

"Be self-controlled and alert. Your enemy the devil prowls around like a roaring lion looking for someone to devour." 1 Peter 5:8

"Submit yourselves, then, to God. Resist the devil ..." James 4:7

3. Remember key facts about the devil and about God

• The devil is a defeated enemy

"The reason the Son of God appeared was to destroy the devil's work." 1 John 3:8

"... he [the devil] will flee from you." James 4:7

• God is stronger than Satan

"The God of peace will soon crush Satan under your feet." Romans 16:20

Bible Promise No. 26

"But the Lord is faithful, and he will strengthen and protect you from the evil one." 2 Thessalonians 3:3

When I worry

Bible Promise No. 27

"Cast all your anxiety on him [God] because he cares for you."
1 Peter 5:7

A command from Jesus

"Do not worry". Jesus said:

"Therefore I tell you, do not worry about your life, what you will eat or drink; or about your body, what you will wear. Is not life more important than food, and the body more important than clothes?"
Matthew 6:25

Learning from the birds

"Look at the birds of the air; they do not sow or reap or store away in barns, and yet your heavenly Father feeds them."
Matthew 6:26

The futility of worry

"Are you not much more valuable than they? Who of you by worrying can add a single hour to his life?" Matthew 6:27

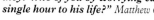

Said the Robin to the Sparrow

Said the Robin to the Sparrow:
**"I should really like to know,
Why these anxious human beings
Rush about and worry so."**

Said the Sparrow to the Robin:
**"Friend, I think it must be,
That they have no heavenly Father
Such as cares for you and me!"**
Author unknown

When I worry

The words of Jesus	What Jesus is teaching
"And why do you worry about clothes?	It is wrong to worry about life's necessities.
"See how the lilies of the field grow. They do not labor or spin. Yet I tell you that not even Solomon in all his splendor was dressed like one of these. If that is how God clothes the grass of the field, which is here today and tomorrow is thrown into the fire, will he not much more clothe you, O you of little faith?	Learn from the wild flowers.
"For the pagans run after all these things,	Worry is sinful. It leaves God out of our life.
"and your heavenly Father knows that you need them.	We have a caring heavenly Father.
"But seek first his kingdom and his righteousness, and all these things will be given to you as well.	Set our sights on God's kingdom.
"Therefore do not worry about tomorrow, for tomorrow will worry about itself. Each day has enough trouble of its own." *Matthew 6:28-34*	Do not worry about the future.

31

Bible Promise No. 28
"The eternal God is your refuge, and underneath are the everlasting arms."
    Deuteronomy 33:27

When to worry
When we see the lilies spinning in distress,
Taking thought to manufacture loveliness;
When we see the birds all building barns for store,
'Twill then be time for us to worry – not before.
    Author unknown

When I think about Heaven

Bible Promise No. 29

"Do not let your hearts be troubled. Trust in God; trust also in me. In my Father's house are many rooms; if it were not so, I would have told you. I am going there to prepare a place for you."

John 14:1-2

Heaven is being with Jesus

[One of the two criminals who was crucified with Jesus] said, *"Jesus, remember me when you come into your kingdom.' Jesus answered him, 'I tell you the truth, today you will be with me in paradise.'"*

Luke 23:43

The glory of heaven

"The glory of heaven consists in the full manifestation of divine wisdom, goodness, grace, holiness – of all the properties of the nature of God in Christ. In the clear perception and constant contemplation hereof consists no small part of eternal blessedness."

John Owen

Perfection

"Heaven will be the perfection we have always longed for. All the things that made earth unlovely and tragic will be absent in heaven."

Billy Graham

Safe into the haven

"Jesus, lover of my soul, let me to Thy bosom fly,
While the nearer waters roll, while the tempest still is high.
Hide me, O my Saviour, hide, till the storm of life is past;
Safe into the haven guide; O receive my soul at last."

Charles Wesley

When I am anxious

A bundle of sticks

"I compare the troubles which we have to undergo in the course of the year to a great bundle of sticks, far too large for us to lift. But God does not require us to carry the whole at once. He mercifully unties the bundle, and gives us first one stick, which we are to carry today, and then another, which we are to carry tomorrow, and so on. This we might easily manage, if we would only take the burden appointed for each day; but we choose to increase our troubles by carrying yesterday's stick over again today, and adding tomorrow's burden to the load, before we are required to bear it."
    John Newton

Bible Promise No. 30

"Cast all your cares on the Lord and he will sustain you; he will never let the righteous fall."
Psalm 55:22

33

Who is carrying your cares?

The psalmist is realist enough to know that we all go around weighed down with our own anxieties. We may know the maxim that: *"Anxiety does not empty tomorrow of its sorrows, but only empties today of its strength."* But, all too often, we remain burdened with worry. The psalmist says that we must take the conscious step of unloading our cares on the Lord. *"Cast all your cares on the Lord."*

Two antidotes to anxiety

1. Prayer
"Pray, and let God worry."
    Martin Luther

2. Trust
"Oh, how great peace and quietness would he possess who should cut off all vain anxiety and place all his confidence in God."
    Thomas à Kempis

When I'm afraid

Bible Promise No. 31

"He will cover you with his feathers, and under his wings you will find refuge; his faithfulness will be your shield and rampart. You will not fear the terror of night, nor the arrow that flies by day."
Psalm 91:4-5

Fear

"F.E.A.R - False Evidence Appearing Real."
Author unknown

"Jesus came treading the waves; and so he puts all the swelling tumults of life under his feet. Christians — why are you afraid?"
Augustine of Hippo

Living without fear

"There is no fear in love. But perfect love drives out fear, because fear has to do with punishment. The one who fears is not made perfect in love."
1 John 4:18

Faith or fear?

*"Fear imprisons, faith liberates;
fear paralyzes, faith empowers;
fear disheartens, faith encourages;
fear sickens, faith heals;
fear makes useless, faith makes serviceable;
most of all, fear puts hopelessness at the heart of life,
while faith rejoices in its God."*
H.E. Fosdick

When I'm afraid

Fear and prayer
"If I could hear Christ praying for me in the next room, I would not fear a million enemies. Yet distance makes no difference. He is praying for me."
  Robert Murray M'Cheyne

Two "fear nots"

1. Fear not, in danger
"'Don't be afraid,' the prophet answered. 'Those who are with us are more than those who are with them.'"
  2 Kings 6:16

2. Fear not, when facing financial problems
"So don't be afraid; you are worth more than many sparrows." Luke 12:32

The right kind of bravery
"A proud and self-reliant man rightly fears to undertake anything, but a humble man becomes all the braver as he realizes his own powerlessness; all the bolder as he sees his own weakness; for all his confidence is in God, who delights to reveal his almighty power in our infirmity and his mercy in our misery."
  Francis de Sales

Bible Promise No. 32
*"So do not fear, for I am with you;
do not be dismayed, for I am your God.
I will strengthen you and help you;
I will uphold you with my righteous right hand."*
Isaiah 41:10

When I'm seeking guidance

Bible Promise No. 33

"Delight yourself in the Lord and he will give you the desires of your heart. Commit your way to the Lord; trust in him and he will do this ..."

Psalm 37:4-5

Conditions for guidance

Many of the Bible promises are dependent on our fulfilling certain conditions.

Three conditions concerning God's guidance mentioned in these verses are:

1. *"Delight yourself in the Lord."*
It is all too easy to become so caught up over the details of guidance that we forget our Guide.

2. *"Commit your way to the Lord."*
"It is morally impossible to exercise trust in God while there is failure to wait upon Him for guidance and direction."
D.E. Hoste

3. *"... trust in him ..."*

The challenge of guidance

"It is not enough to hold that God did great things for our fathers: not enough to pride ourselves on the inheritance of victories of faith: not enough to build the sepulchers of those who were martyred by men unwilling, in their day of trial as we may be in our own, to hear new voices of a living God. Our duty is to see whether God is with us; whether we expect great things from him; whether we do not practically place him far off, forgetting that, if he is, he is about us, speaking to us words that have not been heard before, guiding us to paths on which earlier generations have not been able to enter."
Brooke Foss Westcott

When I'm seeking guidance

1. God's guidance comes through other people
"A wise man has ... many advisers."
  Proverbs 24:5-6

2. God's guidance comes through our conscience as it responds to God's word
Our conscience should be listened to, though it is not infallible and needs to be educated in God's teaching.
"And I will place within them as a guide
    my umpire Conscience,
  whom if they will hear,
Light after light well used they shall
    attain,
And to the end persisting, safe arrive."
  John Milton

3. God's guidance comes from Jesus
"Hang this question up in your houses: 'What would Jesus do?' Then think of another question: 'How would Jesus do it?' For what Jesus would do, and how he would do it, may always stand as the best guide to us."
  C.H. Spurgeon

4. God's guidance comes from prayer
"When we fail to wait prayerfully for God's guidance and strength, we are saying with our actions if not our lips, that we do not need him."
  Charles Hummel

Bible Promise No. 34
"My son, keep your
    father's
    commands
and do not forsake
    your mother's
    teaching. ...
When you walk,
    they will guide
    you;
when you sleep,
    they will watch
    over you;
when you awake,
    they will speak
    to you."
Proverbs 6:20,22

When I'm seeking guidance

Bible Promise No. 35

*"I will instruct you
and teach you in
the way you
should go;
I will counsel you
and watch over
you."*
Psalm 32:8

What are the conditions for God's guidance?

1. To use our God-given minds
*"Do not be like the horse or the mule,
which have no understanding
but must be controlled by bit and bridle
or they will not come to you."*
Psalm 32:9

2. To trust God, not our own understanding
*"Trust in the Lord with all your
heart and lean not on your own
understanding ..."*
Proverbs 3:5

3. To acknowledge God in all we do
*"... in all your ways acknowledge him,
and he will make your paths straight."*
Proverbs 3:6

4. To believe that God is keeping his word and guiding us through things that happen and the promptings of his Word.

God means what he has said
*"There is a living God;
has spoken in the Bible.
He means what he says
and will do all he has promised."*
Hudson Taylor

When I'm seeking guidance

Principles about God's guidance found in the Bible

1. Read the Old Testament and the New Testament

Nobody is guided by the Holy Spirit in a way which is contrary to the clearly-revealed teachings of God in the Bible. We should make ourselves aware of God's teaching which he has given to us in the Bible.

2. Christians should actively seek God's will

Many of the best examples in the Bible, of people seeking God's will, are linked to prayer. If we want to be guided by God we should be praying to him for guidance.

David is an example of a biblical character who looked for guidance in God's Word. *Psalm 19:7-14; 119.*

3. Every Christian is responsible to God

No matter how much help we may receive from other Christians we are each directly responsible to God for discovering his will for our own lives. God has given to each Christian his own Spirit and this Spirit will make known God's will to us.

"The Counselor, the Holy Spirit ... will teach you all things."
   John 14:26

Bible Promise
No. 36
"The Lord will guide you always."
   Isaiah 58:11

When I long for contentment

*"Then Jesus
declared, 'I am the
bread of life. He
who comes to me
will never go
hungry, and he
who believes in me
will never be
thirsty.'"*
John 6:35

Paul's secret
*"... I have learned to be content whatever
the circumstances.
I know what it is to be in need,
and I know what it is to have plenty.
I have learned the secret of being content
in any and every situation,
whether well fed or hungry,
whether living in plenty or in want.
I can do everything through him who
gives me strength."*
Philippians 4:11-13

What do we need to do to be content?
- Come to Jesus in prayer – this is active.
- Firmly believe that Jesus is alive and that his promises are true.
- Reflect on his words and then apply them to our own life. *"The one who feeds on me will live."* John 6:37

All day long
"A man is what he thinks about all day long." Ralph Waldo Emerson

Teresa's Bookmark
*Let nothing disturb you,
nothing frighten you;
All things are passing;
God never changes;
Patient endurance
Attains all things;
Whoever possesses God
Lacks nothing;
God alone suffices.*
Teresa of Avila

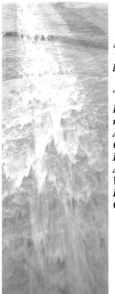

When I'm facing severe trials

Martyrdom

Christian martyrs have not said that God failed them even when they faced being killed. Barbara Youderian, the wife of Roj Youderian who died along with Jim Elliot as they sought to reach the Auca Indians, made the following entry in her diary.

"Tonight, the captain told us of his finding four bodies in the river. One had tee-shirt and blue jeans. Roj was the only one who wore them. ... As I came face to face with the news of Roj's death, my heart was filled with praise. He was worthy of his home-going. Help me, Lord, to be both mommy and daddy."

Bible Promise
No. 38
"... the Lord knows how to rescue godly men from trials ..."
2 Peter 2:9

The shortest way to happiness

"If I could tell you the shortest way to all happiness and perfection, it would be to make a rule for yourself to thank and praise God for everything that happens to you. For it is certain that whatever seeming calamity may happen to you, if you thank and praise God for it, you turn it into a blessing. If you could work miracles you could not do more for yourself than to have this thankful spirit for it heals by just a word and turns all that it touches into happiness."
William Law

A martyr's motto

"He is no fool who gives what he cannot keep to gain what he cannot lose."
Jim Elliott

When I'm broken-hearted

Bible Promise No. 39

"The Lord is close to the broken-hearted and saves those who are crushed in spirit."
Psalm 34:18

The work of Jesus

"The Spirit of the Sovereign Lord is on me,
because the Lord has anointed me
to preach good news to the poor.
He has sent me to bind up the broken-hearted,
to proclaim freedom for the captives
and release from darkness for the prisoners,
to proclaim the year of the Lord's favor
and the day of vengeance of our God,
to comfort all who mourn,
and provide for those who grieve in Zion –
to bestow on them a crown of beauty instead of ashes,
the oil of gladness instead of mourning,
and the garment of praise instead of the spirit of despair.
They will be called oaks of righteousness,
a planting of the Lord
for the display of his splendor."
Isaiah 61:1-3

Trust, even in the most difficult times
Trust the past to God's mercy,
the present to his love,
and the future to his providence.
Augustine of Hippo

When I'm broken-hearted

The Underwood
Like the verses from Isaiah chapter 61, these words were written with the broken-hearted in mind.

Hear me, O God!
A broken heart
Is my best part:
Use still thy rod,
That I may prove
Therein thy love.

If thou hadst not
Been stern to me,
But left me free,
I had forgot
Myself and thee.
  Ben Jonson

Like stars
"God's promises are like the stars; the darker the night the brighter they shine."
  David Nicholas

Bible Promise No. 40
"Your sun will never set again, and your moon will wane no more;
the Lord will be your everlasting light,
and your days of sorrow will end."
Isaiah 60:20

When I need to know that God loves me

Bible Promise No. 41

"For as high as the heavens are above the earth, so great is his love for those who fear him; as far as the east is from the west, so far has he removed our transgressions from us."
Psalm 103:11-12

John 3:16

"For God...	*The greatest lover*
So Loved...	*The greatest degree*
The World...	*The greatest company*
That He Gave...	*The greatest act*
His Only Begotten Son...	*The greatest gift*
That Whosoever...	*The greatest invitation*
Believeth...	*The greatest simplicity*
In Him...	*The greatest attraction*
Should Not Perish...	*The greatest promise*
But...	*The greatest difference*
Have...	*The greatest certainty*
Everlasting Life...	*The greatest possession"*

Author unknown

Like the Amazon
"The love of God is like the Amazon River flowing down to water one daisy."
Author unknown

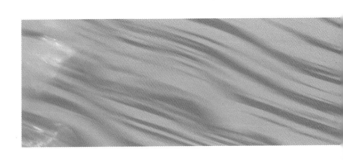

When I'm weighed down

Wings to the soul
According to an old legend, the birds at first had no wings. When wings were given to them the birds rebelled, because they seemed to be a burden. But when the birds accepted their wings, the burden lifted them to the sky.
"The wight of Jesus' yoke is wings to the soul."

Rest
"You have created us for yourself, and our hearts are restless until they find their rest in you."
Augustine of Hippo

Daily
"Praise be to the Lord, to God our
* Savior,*
who daily bears our burdens."
Psalm 68:19

Embracing God's promises
"The main hinge on which faith turns is this: we must not imagine that the Lord's promises are true objectively but not in our experience. We must make them ours by embracing them in our hearts."
John Calvin

"Come to me, all you who are weary and burdened, and I will give you rest. Take my yoke upon you and learn from me, for I am gentle and humble in heart, and you will find rest for your souls. For my yoke is easy and my burden is light."
Matthew 11:28-30

When I pray

Bible Promise No. 43

"Therefore I tell you, whatever you ask for in prayer, believe that you have received it, and it will be yours."

Mark 11:24

Three conditions for answered prayer

1. *"You will seek me and find me when you seek me with all your heart."*
   Jeremiah 29:13
2. *"If I had cherished sin in my heart, the Lord would not have listened."*
   Psalm 66:18
3. *"Faith as small as a mustard seed ..."*
   Matthew 17:20

The Universal Prayer

1.00am *Lord, I believe in you – increase my faith.*
2.00am *I trust in you – strengthen my trust.*
3.00am *I love you – let me love you more and more.*
4.00am *I am sorry for my sins – deepen my sorrow.*
5.00am *I worship you as my first beginning.*
6.00am *I long for you as my last end.*
7.00am *I praise you as my constant helper.*
8.00am *I call on you as my loving protector.*
9.00am *Guide me by your wisdom.*
10.00am *Correct me with your justice.*
11.00am *Comfort me with your mercy.*
Noon *Protect me with your power.*

When I pray

The Universal Prayer (cont'd)

1.00pm I offer you, Lord, my thoughts, my actions and my sufferings.

2.00pm I want to do what you ask of me, in the way you ask, for as long as you ask, because you ask it.

3.00pm Lord, enlighten my understanding, strengthen my will, purify my heart, and make me holy.

4.00pm Help me to repent of my past sins and to resist temptation in the future. Help me rise above my human weaknesses and to grow stronger as a Christian.

5.00pm Let me love you, my Lord and my God, and see myself as I really am, a pilgrim in this world.

6.00pm Help me to conquer anger with gentleness, greed with generosity, apathy by fervor. Help me to forget myself and reach out to others.

7.00pm Make me prudent in planning, courageous in taking risks.

8.00pm Make me patient in suffering, unassuming in prosperity.

9.00pm Keep me, Lord, attentive at prayer, temperate in food and drink, diligent in my work, firm in my good intentions.

10.00pm Let my conscience be clear, my conduct without fault, my speech blameless, and my life well-ordered.

11.00pm Teach me to realize that this world is passing, that my true future is the happiness of heaven, that life on earth is short, and the life to come eternal.

Midnight Help me prepare for death with a proper fear of judgment, and a greater trust in your goodness. Lead me safely through death to the endless joy of heaven. Grant this through Christ our Lord. Amen.

The Universal Prayer, attributed to Clement XI

Bible Promise No. 44

"So I say to you: Ask and it will be given to you; seek and you will find; knock and the door will be opened to you. For everyone who asks receives; he who seeks finds; and to him who knocks, the door will be opened."

Luke 11:9-10

47

When I think about dying

Bible Promise No. 45

"I am the resurrection and the life. He who believes in me will live, even though he dies; and whoever lives and believes in me will never die."

John 11:25-26

Abide with me
H.F. Lyte wrote this hymn on the evening of Sunday 4th, 1847, in Lower Brixham, Devon, England, as he sensed his own impending death. He died two weeks later.

Abide with me; fast falls the eventide;
The darkness deepens; Lord, with me
abide!
When other helpers fail, and comforts
flee,
Help of the helpless, O abide with me.

Swift to its close ebbs out life's little day;
Earth's joys grow dim, its glories pass
away;
Change and decay in all around I see;
O thou who changest not, abide with me.

I need thy presence every passing hour;
What but thy grace can foil the tempter's
power?
Who like thyself my guide and stay can be?
Through cloud and sunshine, O abide with
me.

I fear no foe with thee at hand to bless;
Ills have no weight, and tears no
bitterness.
Where is death's sting? where, grave, thy
victory?
I triumph still, if thou abide with me.

Hold thou thy cross before my closing
eyes;
Shine through the gloom, and point me to
the skies:
Heaven's morning breaks, and earth's
vain shadows flee;
In life, in death, O Lord, abide with me!
H.F. Lyte

When I look at my spiritual life

Stances to emulate in our spiritual lives

1. As we lie down: lie down for spiritual refreshment
"He makes me lie down in green pastures." Psalm 23:2

2. As we sit: sit to receive God's instructions
"Mary ... sat at the Lord's feet, listening to what he said." Luke 10:39

3. As we stand: stand to resist Satan
"Stand firm then ..." Ephesians 6:14

4. As we walk: walk in Christian fellowship
"But if we walk in the light, as he is in the light, was have fellowship with one another." 1 John 1:7

5. As we run: run to make progress
"... let us run with perseverance the race marked out for us." Hebrews 12:1

6. As we leap: leap for ecstacy
"... walking and jumping, and praising God." Acts 3:8

7. As we soar: soar with renewed strength
"They will soar on wings like eagles." Isaiah 40:31

Bible Promise No. 46

"Now to him who is able to do immeasurably more than all we ask or imagine, according to his power that is at work within us, to him be glory in the church and in Christ Jesus throughout all generations, for ever and ever! Amen."
Ephesians 3:20-21

When I want peace with God

Bible Promise No. 47

"Therefore, since we have been justified through faith, we have peace with God through our Lord Jesus Christ ... But God demonstrates his love for us in this: While we were still sinners, Christ died for us."

Romans 5:1,8

Peace, peace, peace
"Christ alone can bring lasting peace:
peace with God;
peace among men and nations;
and peace within our hearts."
  Billy Graham

Peace
"I was in Chelsea police station where I was charged with perjury and conspiracy to pervert public justice. I spent the next five hours alone in a police cell while waiting for the various formalities such as finger-printing and photographs. I used that time to pray, to meditate and to read all sixteen chapters of St Mark's Gospel, something I had long meant to do at one sitting. This should have been a time of deep despair. The worst day of my life. Not so. For I had such an overwhelming sense of God's presence in the cell with me that I was at peace."
  Jonathan Aitken, former member of the British Cabinet, imprisoned for perjury

Knowing peace
"No God, no peace.
Know God, know peace."
  Author Unknown

When I fear being separated from God

God's words from Romans 8:38-39 applied to our lives

"neither death nor life,	Death has been "swallowed up in victory." *1 Corinthians 15:54* Life is the place for Christian service.
neither angels nor demons,	The hostile or potentially hostile forces behind the material universe have been stripped of their powers.
neither the present nor the future,	Today and tomorrow are in God's hands.
nor any powers,	Jesus is "stronger than the strong," and so overcomes all evil powers.
neither height nor depth,	Height and depth were astrological terms for the highest and lowest points reached by the stars. In Paul's day people believed that their lives were controlled by the position of the stars. Paul says that such fears are groundless for the Christian. It is impossible to be beyond God's loving reach.
nor anything else in all creation,	God created the world and remains in control of his creation.
will be able to separate us from the love of God	No passing troubles need come between us and God's eternal love for us.
that is in Christ Jesus our Lord."	When we want to view God's love we focus on Jesus.

Bible Promise No. 48

"For I am convinced that neither death nor life, neither angels nor demons, neither the present nor the future, nor any powers, neither height nor depth, nor anything else in all creation, will be able to separate us from the love of God that is in Christ Jesus our Lord."
   Romans 8:38-39

When I want to know for certain about my salvation

Bible Promise No. 49

"And this is the testimony: God has given us eternal life, and this life is in his Son. He who has the Son has life; he who does not have the Son does not have life. I write these things to you who believe in the name of the Son of God so that you may know that you have eternal life."

1 John 5: 11-13

52

Reflect on God's promises

"When reflecting on God promises faith must fight a long and bitter fight, for reason or the flesh judges that God's promises are impossible. Therefore faith must battle against reason and its doubts."

Martin Luther

Martin Luther's prayer about assurance

"Dear Lord, although I am sure of my position, I am unable to sustain it without you. Help me or I am lost."

Martin Luther

The tenses of God's presence

"Yesterday, God was very gracious to me;
tomorrow he will be very gracious to me;
and the same will be true the next day, and the next day,
and the next day, until there shall be no more days,
and time shall be swallowed up in eternity."

C.H. Spurgeon

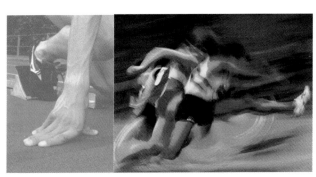

When I need to be patient

53

"Wait patiently"

"I wish we Christians could learn, like the author of Psalm 40, to 'Wait patiently for the Lord.'" John Stott

Consider God's promises

Consider the promises of God. Most of them have no time-clause attached to them. God promises that he will do something and not when he will do it.

For example, Abraham, Isaac and Jacob did not, themselves, inherit the Promised Land. They died in faith not having received the promise. *See Hebrews 11:13.* The promise was inherited by their descendants. It was only centuries later that "God remembered his covenant" (*Exodus 2:24*), and delivered Israel from Egypt in fulfilment of his ancient promise. It is a great mistake to suppose that God's promises are inherited by faith alone; they are inherited by faith and patience. *See Hebrews 6:12*

Bible Promise No. 50

"I waited patiently for the Lord; he turned to me and heard my cry. He lifted me out of the slimy pit, out of the mud and mire; he set my feet on a rock and gave me a firm place to stand."
Psalm 40:1-2

When I think about old age

Bible Promise No. 51

"The righteous will flourish like a palm tree, they will grow like a cedar of Lebanon; planted in the house of the Lord, they will flourish in the courts of our God. They will still bear fruit in old age, they will stay fresh and green, proclaiming, 'The Lord is upright; he is my Rock, and there is no wickedness in him'"
Psalm 92:12-15

As we grow weaker

In old age, our bodies and minds may grow weaker, but our spirits should grow stronger, shining with God's glory.
"And we who with unveiled faces all reflect the Lord's glory, are being transformed into his likeness with ever-increasing glory, which comes from the Lord, who is the Spirit." 2 Corinthians 3:18

The example of an 84 year old widow

"There was also a prophetess, Anna, a daughter of Phanuel, of the tribe of Asher. She was very old; she had lived with her husband seven years after her marriage, and then was a widow until she was eighty-four. She never left the temple but worshiped night and day, fasting and praying." Luke 2:36-37

O for a closer walk with God

O for a closer walk with God,
A calm and heavenly frame;
A light to shine upon the road
That leads me to the Lamb!
   William Cowper

When I think about old age

Advice for us when our faculties are failing

Paul wrote these words when he was being attacked from all sides. They apply to us when we feel that we are about to "lose heart".

The words of Paul	An application for us
"Therefore we do not lose heart.	There are good reasons for not giving up.
"Though outwardly we are wasting away, yet inwardly we are being renewed.	Outward aging can be matched by inner renewal.
"For our light and momentary troubles are achieving for us an eternal glory that far outweighs them all.	When looked at in the light of eternity our present troubles are put into perspective.
"So we fix our eyes not on what is seen, but on what is unseen.	Where we direct our attention will determine the kind of day we have today.
"For what is seen is temporary, but what is unseen is eternal." 2 Corinthians 4:16-18	Try to reflect on invisible spiritual realities.

Mind over matter

"Set your minds on the things above, not on earthly things." Colossians 3:2

Bible Promise No. 52

"Blessed is the man who trusts in the Lord, whose confidence is in him. He will be like a tree planted by the water that sends out its roots by the stream. It does not fear when heat comes; its leaves are always green. It has no worries in a year of drought and never fails to bear fruit." Jeremiah 17:7-8

When I want to lead a godly life

Bible Promise No. 53

"His divine power has given us everything we need for life and godliness through our knowledge of him who called us by his own glory and goodness. Through these he has given us his very great and precious promises, so that through them you may participate in the divine nature and escape the corruption in the world caused by evil desires."

2 Peter 1:3-4

Godliness is ...

Godly people are those who trust God completely and express their trust in obedience.

"The person who has godliness lacks nothing. Godliness is the beginning, middle and end of Christian living, and, where it is completed, nothing is lacking."

John Calvin, from his commentary 1 Timothy

Praising God leads to godliness

"Praise to the Holiest in the height, And in the depth be praise; In all his words most wonderful, Most sure in all his ways."

J.H. Newman

The foundation of our faith

"God's promises are a foundation of our faith, and we have them as such; and also of our hope. On these we are to build all our expectations from God."

Matthew Henry

Godliness is impossible without trusting God

"All God's giants have been weak men, who did great things for God because they believed that God would be with them."

Hudson Taylor

When I want to grow spiritually

A spiritual ABC

Ask the Father daily in prayer and He will answer.

BELIEVE!

Christ must be the center of your life.

Dare to be a Disciple of Jesus.

Even you can make a difference in the lives of others by acting out God's will in your daily life.

Friends are special gifts from God.

Give to others cheerfully.

Harmony is what you should strive for in your relationships with others.

Interest in others will make you a broader minded person.

Judge others with love and compassion.

Knowledge and wisdom come from the Lord.

Live in such a way that those who know you but don't know God will come to know God because they know you.

Make sure to always love others as Jesus does.

New life comes to you when you accept Christ.

Obedience of God's will leads to God's blessings.

Please God in all of your actions.

Question your priorities often. Make sure **G**od always comes first.

Read God's Word daily.

Shepherds protect the sheep, and I am grateful that the Lord is my shepherd.

Talk with God often.

Use your heart to show concern for others.

Vent feelings, but always with the love of Christ.

E**X**alt the Lord always!

Yesterday's sins are already paid for by the grace of Jesus Christ.

Zeal in living my spiritual ABCs will help me grow in the Lord.

Author unknown

Bible Promise No. 54

"He who began a good work in you will carry it on to completion until the day of Christ Jesus."

Philippians 1:6

When I need to feel God's favor on me

Our thinking	God's promise
It's impossible	All things are possible *(Luke 18:27)*
I'm too tired	I will give you rest *(Matthew 11:28-30)*
Nobody really loves me	I love you *(John 3:16; John 13:34)*
1 can't go on	My grace is sufficient *(2 Corinthians 12:9)*
I can't figure things out	I will direct your steps *(Proverbs 3:5-6)*
I can't do it	You can do all things in me *(Philippians 4:13)*
I'm not able	I am able *(I Corinthians 9:8)*
It's not worth it	It will be worth it *(Romans 8:28)*
I can't forgive myself	I forgive you *(I John 1:9)*
I can't manage	I will supply all your needs *(Philippians 4:19)*
I'm afraid	I have not given you a spirit of timidity *(2 Timothy 1:7)*
I'm always worried and frustrated	Cast all your anxiety on me *(I Peter 5:7)*
I don't have enough faith	I've given everyone a measure of faith *(Romans 12:3)*
I'm not smart enough	I give you wisdom *(I Corinthians 1:30)*
I feel all alone	I will never leave you or forsake you *(Hebrews 13:5)*

Author unknown

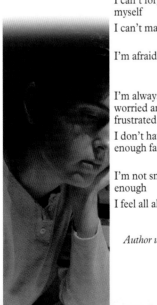

When I doubt God's love

Love bade me welcome

Love bade me welcome: yet my soul drew
*   back,*
Guilty of dust and sin.
But quick-ey'd Love, observing me grow
*   slack*
From my first entrance in,
Drew nearer to me, sweetly questioning,
If I lack'd any thing.

A guest, I answer'd, worthy to be here:
Love said, You shall be he.
I the unkind, ungrateful? Ah my dear,
I cannot look on thee.
Love took my hand, and smiling did
*   reply,*
Who made the eyes but I?

Truth Lord, but I have marr'd them: let
*   my shame*
Go where it doth deserve.
And know you not, says Love, who bore
*   the blame?*
My dear, then I will serve.
You must sit down, says Love, and taste
*   my meat:*
So I did sit and eat.
  George Herbert

Bible Promise No. 56

"The Lord watches
*   over you—*
the Lord is your
*   shade at your*
*   right hand;*
the sun will not
*   harm you by*
*   day,*
*   nor the moon by*
*   night.*
The Lord will keep
*   you from all*
*   ·harm—*
he will watch
*   over your life."*
Psalm 121:5-7

When I'm under great stress

Bible Promise No. 57

[Moses said], "Be strong and courageous. Do not be afraid or terrified because of them, for the Lord your God goes with you; he will never leave you nor forsake you."
Deuteronomy 31:6

Remember, you are loved by God
"Say to yourself: 'I am loved by God more than I can either conceive or understand.' Let this fill all your soul and never leave you. You will see that this is the way to find God."
   Henri de Tourville

Surviving under stress
Paul knew more about severe pressure than most of us.
*"I have ... been
in prison more frequently,
been flogged more severely,
and been exposed to death again and
   again.
Five times I received from the Jews the
   forty lashes minus one.
Three times I was beaten with rods,
once I was stoned ..."*
   2 Corinthians 11:23-25

The Lord stood by me
"At my first defense, no one came to my support, but everyone deserted me. May it not be held against them. But the Lord stood at my side and gave me strength, so that through me the message might be fully proclaimed and all the Gentiles might hear it. And I was delivered from the lion's mouth." 2 Timothy 4:16-17

Faithful Luke
Sometimes you may find that you are the only person to support a Christian friend.
"Only Luke is with me." 2 Timothy 4:11

When I can't sleep because of stress

All your trust
"Set all your trust in God and fear not the language of the world; for the more despite, shame, and reproof that you receive in the world, the more is your merit in the sight of God."
Julian of Norwich

When human helpers fail
"The acid test of our faith in the promises of God is never found in the easy-going, comfortable ways of life, but in the great emergencies, the times of storm and of stress, the days of adversity, when all human aid fails."
Ethel Bell

Either ... or ...
"Do not look forward to the changes and chances of this life in fear; rather look to them with full hope that, as they arise, God, whose you are, will deliver you out of them. He is your keeper. He has kept you hitherto. Do you but hold fast to his dear hand, and he will lead you safely through all things; and, when you cannot stand, he will bear you in his arms. Do not look forward to what may happen tomorrow. Our Father will either shield you from suffering, or he will give you strength to bear it."
Francis of Sales

Promises of God
"Tackle life's problems by trusting God's promises." *Author unknown*

Bible Promise No. 58
"... when you lie down, you will not be afraid; when you lie down, your sleep will be sweet. Have no fear of sudden disaster or of the ruin that overtakes the wicked, for the Lord will be your confidence and will keep your foot from being snared."
Proverbs 3:24-26

When I'm weak

Bible Promise No. 59

"Three times I pleaded with the Lord to take it [a thorn in my flesh, a messenger of Satan] away from me. But he said to me, 'My grace is sufficient for you, for my power is make perfect in weakness.'"

2 Corinthians 12:8-9

He that is low

He that is down needs fear no fall
He that is low, no pride:
He that is humble ever shall
Have God to be his guide.

I am content with what I have,
Little be it or much:
And, Lord, contentment still I crave,
Because thou savest such.

John Bunyan, Pilgrim's Progress

Weakness

"... the Spirit helps us in our weakness ..." Romans 8:26

Divine sympathy in our weakness

"For we do not have a high priest who is unable to sympathize with our weaknesses ..." Hebrews 4:15

When I need to pray

Do you have a prayerful soul?
"There are moments when whatever be the attitude of the body, the soul is on its knees."

Author unknown

An explorer's journal
"He will keep His word – the gracious One, full of grace and truth; no doubt of it. He said, 'Him that cometh unto Me, I will in no wise cast out'; and 'Whatsoever ye shall ask in My name, I will give it.' He will keep his word; then I can come and humbly present my petition and it will be all right. Doubt is here inadmissible, surely."

David Livingstone's Journal, May 13th, 1872

Prayer displays our trust in God
"Every thing that a man leans upon but God, will be a dart that will certainly pierce his heart through and through. He, who leans only upon Christ, lives the highest, choicest, safest, and sweetest life."

Thomas Brooks

Bible Promise No. 60
"Ask and it will be given to you; seek and you will find; knock and the door will be opened to you. For everyone who asks receives; he who seeks finds; and to him who knocks, the door will be opened."

Matthew 7:7-8

When I read the Bible

Bible Promise No. 61

"Your word is a lamp to my feet and a light to my path."
Psalm 119:108

The Bible can be trusted

"You have been born again, not of perishable seed, but of imperishable, through the living and enduring word of God." 1 Peter 2:23

All the Bible is inspired by God

God designed the Bible:

• to give us hope
"... so that through endurance and the encouragement of the Scriptures we might have hope." Romans 15:4

• to make us holy
"... to make her [the Christian church] holy, cleansing her by the washing with water through the word." Ephesians 5:26

• to make us rejoice
"Your statutes are my heritage forever; they are the joy of my heart."
Psalm 119:111

• to produce faith in us
"Consequently, faith comes from hearing the message, and the message is heard through the word of Christ." Romans 10:17

• to build us up
"Like newborn babes, crave pure spiritual milk, so that by it you may grow up in your salvation." 1 Peter 2:2